The Human Skeleton

Richard Walker

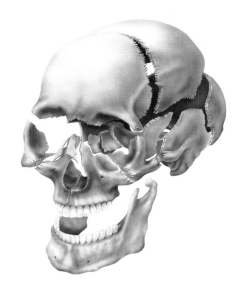

This edition 2007

Franklin Watts
338 Euston Road, London NW1 3BH

Franklin Watts Australia
Level 17/207 Kent Street
Sydney, NSW 2000

Copyright © Franklin Watts 2004

Series editor: Adrian Cole
Series design: White Design
Art director: Jonathan Hair
Picture research: Diana Morris
Educational consultant: Peter Riley
Medical consultant: Dr Gabrielle Murphy

A CIP catalogue record for this book is available from the British Library.

ISBN–13: 978 0 7496 7254 6

Printed in Malaysia

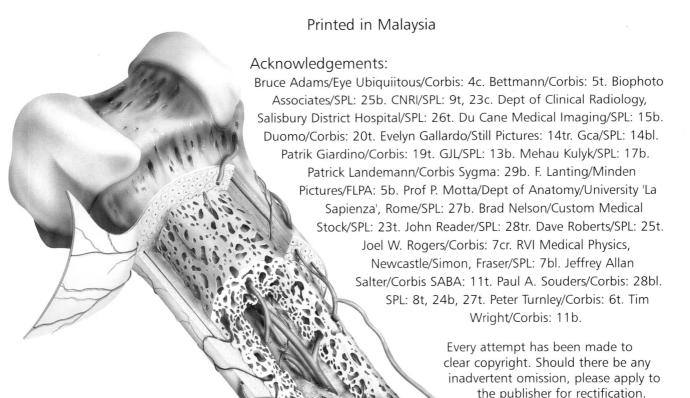

Acknowledgements:
Bruce Adams/Eye Ubiquiitous/Corbis: 4c. Bettmann/Corbis: 5t. Biophoto Associates/SPL: 25b. CNRI/SPL: 9t, 23c. Dept of Clinical Radiology, Salisbury District Hospital/SPL: 26t. Du Cane Medical Imaging/SPL: 15b. Duomo/Corbis: 20t. Evelyn Gallardo/Still Pictures: 14tr. Gca/SPL: 14bl. Patrik Giardino/Corbis: 19t. GJL/SPL: 13b. Mehau Kulyk/SPL: 17b. Patrick Landemann/Corbis Sygma: 29b. F. Lanting/Minden Pictures/FLPA: 5b. Prof P. Motta/Dept of Anatomy/University 'La Sapienza', Rome/SPL: 27b. Brad Nelson/Custom Medical Stock/SPL: 23t. John Reader/SPL: 28tr. Dave Roberts/SPL: 25t. Joel W. Rogers/Corbis: 7cr. RVI Medical Physics, Newcastle/Simon, Fraser/SPL: 7bl. Jeffrey Allan Salter/Corbis SABA: 11t. Paul A. Souders/Corbis: 28bl. SPL: 8t, 24b, 27t. Peter Turnley/Corbis: 6t. Tim Wright/Corbis: 11b.

Every attempt has been made to clear copyright. Should there be any inadvertent omission, please apply to the publisher for rectification.

Franklin Watts is a division of Hachette Children's Books.

Contents

The skeleton is a living framework that
shapes and supports

The skeleton is a living framework inside the body and is made up of bones that are strong and light. The skeleton supports us but also lets us move. It also surrounds the softer parts of the body and helps to stop them being injured.

Bony skeleton

The human skeleton, by the time it is fully formed in the teenage years, is made up of around 206 bones of different shapes and sizes. These bones link together to form the skeleton, which shapes the body. The skeleton surrounds and protects important organs, such as the brain and heart, and also anchors the muscles that pull on the bones. This allows us to walk, run, jump and perform hundreds of other movements.

Bony frame

The skeleton supports the body like the poles of a tent and gives the body shape.

Supporting framework

Gently tap on the skin covering your head. Or squeeze your fingers. What do you feel? It is the bones under the skin and muscles that support your body. But what would happen if they were not there? Without the support of the skeleton's bony framework, the body would collapse into a shapeless heap, a bit like a tent with its tent poles removed.

Skull
surrounds and protects the brain

Clavicle
(collarbone) attaches to the sternum and scapula

Sternum
(breastbone)

Humerus
the longest bone in the arm

Scapula
(shoulder blade)

Ribs
form the protective ribcage

Backbone
(spine) is made of small bones called vertebrae

Pelvis

Metacarpal
is one of 27 bones in the hand

Femur
is the longest bone in the body

Tibia
(shinbone)

Patella
(kneecap) is a piece of bone that protects the knee joint

Tarsal
is one of a group of 26 foot bones

Human skeleton

This view shows most of the bones found in the skeleton.

MYSTERIOUS RAYS

In 1895, a German scientist called Wilhelm Roentgen became the first person to detect invisible rays. They were so mysterious he called them 'X-rays'. Roentgen's X-rays produced an image on a photographic plate that showed bones really clearly. This is because they pass through soft body parts, such as skin and muscle, but not through hard areas, such as bone. For the first time, doctors could find out whether bones inside a living body were damaged or diseased without cutting it open.

Wilhelm Roentgen

The scientist who discovered X-rays at work in his laboratory.

Sting in the tail

This scorpion does not have a skeleton like ours. Instead, it has a thick exoskeleton made up of flexible 'plates' that cover most of its body.

Inside and outside

Animals, such as cats, birds, snakes and fish, have a hard skeleton like ours inside the body. But that is not the only type of skeleton. Other animals – including insects, crabs and scorpions – have an external skeleton called an exoskeleton, which supports and protects the body like a suit of armour.

The skeleton can be divided into
two main parts

There are great variations in the size and shape of the skeleton's bones. Some bones fit together to form the skeleton's central axis, which holds the body upright. Other bones form the arms and legs, as well as the girdles (rings of bone), which attach the arms and legs to the axis, and allow them to move freely.

Two parts

The structure of the skeleton can be divided into two parts. The axial skeleton – the axis or core – consists of the skull, backbone, ribs and sternum. These form the central supporting frame of the skeleton, as well as protecting delicate organs, such as the brain and heart.

The appendicular skeleton is made up of the arm and leg bones, and the girdles in the shoulder and hips, which attach them to the axial skeleton.

Living frame

The axial skeleton keeps these soldiers upright, while the appendicular skeleton allows them to walk and swing their arms.

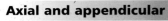

Axial and appendicular

The axial skeleton is shown here in cream, while the appendicular skeleton is coloured blue.

Bone variations

Bones vary in shape and size depending on the job each one does. But all bones fall into one of four groups. Long bones in the arms and legs, which are longer than they are wide, help us move. Short bones make up the wrists and ankles. Flat bones, often curved, such as the skull bones and ribs, protect internal organs. Irregular bones, each with its own complex shape, include the vertebrae of the backbone.

Different types

These are examples of the different types of bones found in the skeleton.

Long bone
for example, the
femur (thigh bone)

Short bone
for example,
a wrist bone

Flat bone
for example, a parietal
bone of the skull

Irregular bone
for example, a
vertebra

Largest and smallest

There are huge differences in size between the largest and the smallest bones in the body. The largest (up to 50 centimetres long in adults) is a long bone called the femur. It is found in the thigh or upper leg and is long and strong because it has to support the body's weight when we stand or move. The smallest (5 millimetres long) is an irregular bone called the stirrup. It is shaped like a horse rider's stirrup and is located inside the ear to help us hear sounds.

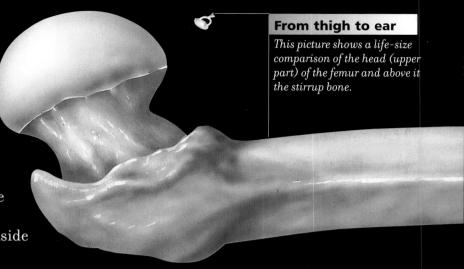

This picture shows a life-size comparison of the head (upper part) of the femur and above it the stirrup bone.

SYMBOLS OF DEATH

Bones and teeth are the only parts of the human body to remain after a person has died and their flesh has rotted away. It is not surprising, then, that for thousands of years, and all around the world, the skeleton has been used as a symbol to represent all sorts of bad events, from death and disease to danger and destruction.

Scanning the skeleton

Apart from X-rays, doctors have other ways of looking at bones. One of these is a radionuclide scan. A radioactive substance is injected into a person, which makes their bones give off rays. These are detected outside the body by a special camera and turned into a colour picture.

Radionuclide scanning

The different colours and patterns in these scans help doctors to work out if bones are damaged or diseased.

The structure of bones makes them
strong and light

A living bone is six times stronger than a piece of steel of the same weight! The combination of strength with lightness in weight is a result of the unique structure of bone. Each one has a very hard, heavy outer layer, with an inner layer that is much lighter, but still strong.

Inside a long bone

Bones are dense towards the outside, but more light and sponge-like further in. Bone tissue is made up of two components – calcium phosphate to make it hard, and fibres of collagen, to make it strong and slightly flexible. In the centre of a long bone is a cavity that contains bone marrow (see below). All bones act as a store of calcium.

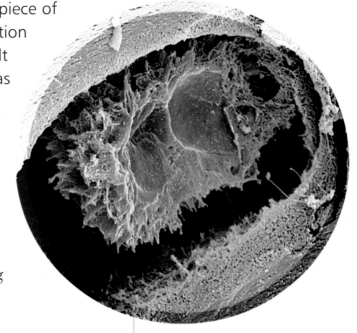

Compact bone
(the outer layer) gives the bone its strength

Bone structure
This picture shows the structure of a long bone, such as the femur.

Bone cell
This micrograph shows a section cut through an osteon showing the space containing a bone cell or osteocyte.

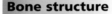

Compact bone

A bone's strength comes from the dense outer layer of compact bone, the body's second hardest material after tooth enamel. Compact bone is made up of microscopic tubes called osteons, which are only 1 millimetre across. They are packed together along a bone, making it strong. Each osteon consists of circular layers of bone tissue. Between these layers are tiny spaces where cells called osteocytes keep bone tissue in good working order.

Osteon
is a long tube of bone tissue

Spongy bone
(the inner layer) gives the bone its lightness

Yellow bone marrow
is a store of energy-rich fat inside the central cavity of a long bone

Blood vessel

Spongy bone

The skeleton would be too heavy if the entire bone was made of compact bone. Inside, bone is a honeycomb-like network of struts called spongy bone. Spongy bone reduces the weight of each bone because it contains spaces, while the struts make it very strong.

Bone marrow

This soft, jelly-like material comes in two types: red and yellow marrow. Red marrow makes the red and white cells that are found in the blood. In young children, red marrow is found in the spongy tissue and cavities of all bones. But as we get older, it is replaced in the cavities of limb bones by yellow marrow, which stores energy-rich fat.

Making blood cells

This micrograph shows newly-produced red and white blood cells. In adults, the production of blood cells occurs mainly in the red marrow in the spongy bone of the skull, ribs, collarbones, shoulder blades, backbone and hipbones.

BONE STRENGTH

Find out how bones get their strength by trying this simple activity. Take a disc of modelling clay and stick about 20 drinking straws into it so they point upwards. Gather the straws together with tape to form a bundle of parallel straws. Press downwards on this bundle using, for example, the flat surface of a book. Unlike a single straw, the bundle of straws does not buckle because together the parallel straws possess lots of strength – just like the osteons in compact bone.

Strong support

This bundle of straws is supporting the weight of the book just like the osteons in bone support the weight of the body.

The skull protects the brain and eyes, **and shapes the face**

The skull is not a single bone, but a complex arrangement of several different bones. It surrounds and protects the brain, eyes, ears, nose and tongue. The skull also gives the head and face its shape, and forms the mouth – the opening through which we take in food and drink.

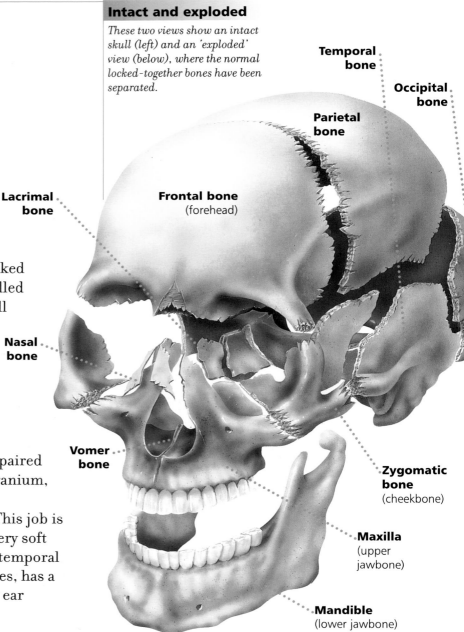

Intact and exploded

These two views show an intact skull (left) and an 'exploded' view (below), where the normal locked-together bones have been separated.

Temporal bone

Occipital bone

Parietal bone

Frontal bone (forehead)

Lacrimal bone

Nasal bone

Vomer bone

Zygomatic bone (cheekbone)

Maxilla (upper jawbone)

Mandible (lower jawbone)

Skull structure

A total of 22 flat and irregular bones make up the skull. All but one – the lower jaw – are tightly locked together by jagged-edged joints, called sutures. This design makes the skull very strong, which is vital for protecting the brain and the sense organs. Skull bones are divided into two types: cranial bones and facial bones.

Brain case

A total of eight cranial bones – two paired and four unpaired – make up the cranium, the part of the skull that supports, surrounds and protects the brain. This job is important because brain tissue is very soft and could be easily damaged. Each temporal bone, one of the paired cranial bones, has a passageway that contains three tiny ear bones that help us hear sounds.

Face former

Fourteen facial bones – six paired and two unpaired – provide the framework that forms and shapes the face. They also provide attachment points for the muscles that pull on the skin and allow us to show a wide range of facial expressions. The upper jaw – formed by the two maxillae – and the lower jaw make up the mouth and carry the teeth. The lower jaw, or mandible, is the only skull bone that can move, allowing the mouth to open and close. Together, facial and cranial bones form the eye and nose cavities that house the sense organs for sight and smell.

Pierced ear

The piercings in the upper ear have been put through flexible cartilage.

Nose and ears

Two prominent features of the head – the ears and most of the nose – are supported and shaped not by bone, but instead by another component of the skeleton called cartilage. Cartilage is flexible, not hard like bone, but it is still very tough. Cartilage also covers the ends of bones in joints (see page 20) and connects the ends of ribs to the sternum (see page 13).

Cartilage framework

Several pieces of cartilage support and shape the nose, giving it the flexibility to wrinkle up.

EXTRA PROTECTION

Your skull is tough, but a sudden blow, for example your head hitting the ground, could crack it or break it open. This is very dangerous because it might damage your brain. That is why extra protection, in the form of a helmet, may be required in certain situations such as riding a bicycle, or during dangerous sports such as rock climbing.

Rock climbing

Wearing extra protection on your head makes sense – your skull is tough, but it can still be damaged by a fall.

The backbone and ribs form the
core of the skeleton

The backbone is a flexible, bony column that runs down the back and supports the head and the trunk – the central part of the body. Twelve pairs of ribs curve round from the backbone towards the front of the chest. The ribs protect organs, such as the heart, inside the chest and help us breathe.

Backbone

The backbone, or 'spine', holds us upright and allows us to bend. It consists of a chain of irregularly-shaped bones called vertebrae. The joints between vertebrae only allow a little movement, but together they make the backbone very flexible.

Cartilage discs

Between each pair of vertebrae there are pieces of cartilage called intervertebral discs. These have a tough outside and a jelly-like inside that allows vertebrae to move, and for us to twist and bend.

'S'-shaped support

This side view of the backbone shows the four curves, plus the 'tail', that give it an 'S' shape:
1. Seven cervical vertebrae run down the neck.
2. Twelve thoracic vertebrae lie behind the ribcage in the chest.
3. Five lumbar vertebrae support the body's weight in the lower back.
4. Sacrum is formed from five fused vertebrae.
5. Coccyx or 'tail' is formed from four fused vertebrae.

Vertebrae

There are 26 vertebrae in the backbone. Despite differences in size, all vertebrae have the same parts: a short pillar-like centrum bears weight; a ring shaped arch forms a tunnel, which protects the spinal cord; and 'spines' provide attachment points for muscles that hold the backbone upright.

Cartilage cushions

Intervertebral discs (one is shown above, coloured purple) help us to bend and also cushion the vertebrae from serious jolts when we run or jump.

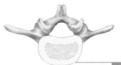

Different types

(From left to right). Top views of lumbar, cervical and thoracic vertebrae.

1.

2.

3.

4.

5.

Ribs and sternum

Most people have 12 pairs of ribs (a few have more or less) that curve round from the backbone, with ten pairs joining the sternum (breastbone) at the front. There are seven pairs of 'true' ribs and five pairs of 'false' ribs (two of these pairs are 'floating' ribs). At the back, each rib forms a movable joint (see pages 22–23) with a thoracic vertebra. Muscles between the ribs, called intercostal muscles, move the ribs up and down to help move air into and out of the lungs during breathing.

Protective cage

Together the ribs, the backbone and the sternum form a protective cage – called the ribcage – that surrounds and protects some of the body's most delicate and important organs. These include the heart and two lungs in the thorax (chest), and the liver, kidneys and stomach in the upper abdomen.

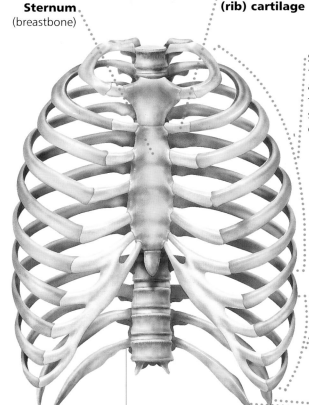

Sternum (breastbone)

Flexible costal (rib) cartilage

Seven pairs of 'true' ribs are connected at their front ends to the sternum by flexible costal (rib) cartilages

Three pairs of 'false' ribs are connected to the 'true' ribs above

Two pairs of 'false' ribs are called 'floating ribs' – they are only connected to the backbone

Ribcage
The different types of ribs attach to the backbone and sternum in different ways.

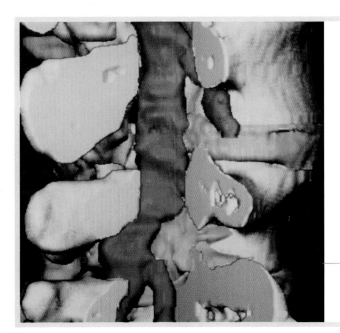

SLIPPED DISC

Sometimes the soft centre of one of the discs between a pair of vertebrae bulges out through the cartilage layer that surrounds it. This is often called a 'slipped disc', even though the disc has not really slipped. The bulging part causes problems because it often presses on the spinal cord or on the spinal nerves. This causes a lot of pain in the back, or pain and a feeling of numbness in the arms or legs.

Disc problem
This scan shows a 'slipped disc' (yellow, lower centre) pressing on the spinal cord (blue).

The hand, arm and shoulder bones form
the upper limb

Using the arms and hands, we are able to perform a wide range of activities, from painting to lifting heavy weights. We can do this because our arms and hands are very flexible. Also, the shoulder joint allows the arm to move in nearly all directions.

Pectoral girdle

A girdle is a ring of bone that anchors limbs to the skeleton. The pectoral (shoulder) girdle anchors the arms. Each side of the pectoral girdle consists of a scapula (shoulder blade) and a clavicle (collarbone). The head (top) of the humerus fits into a hollow in one corner of the triangular scapula.

Anchoring the arm
This coloured X-ray of the shoulder shows how the rounded head of the humerus fits into a socket in the scapula to form a free-moving ball-and-socket joint (see page 22).

Standing tall
Unlike orang-utans and other mammal relatives, humans walk on two legs not four. This has freed our arms and hands to perform all sorts of tasks.

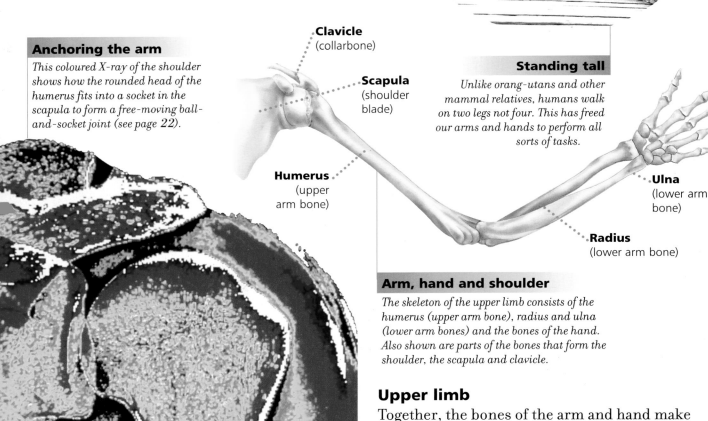

Clavicle (collarbone)

Scapula (shoulder blade)

Humerus (upper arm bone)

Ulna (lower arm bone)

Radius (lower arm bone)

Arm, hand and shoulder
The skeleton of the upper limb consists of the humerus (upper arm bone), radius and ulna (lower arm bones) and the bones of the hand. Also shown are parts of the bones that form the shoulder, the scapula and clavicle.

Upper limb

Together, the bones of the arm and hand make up what is called the upper limb. The flexible arrangement of arm bones allows the arm to be folded up next to the body or extended in order to point or grasp objects.

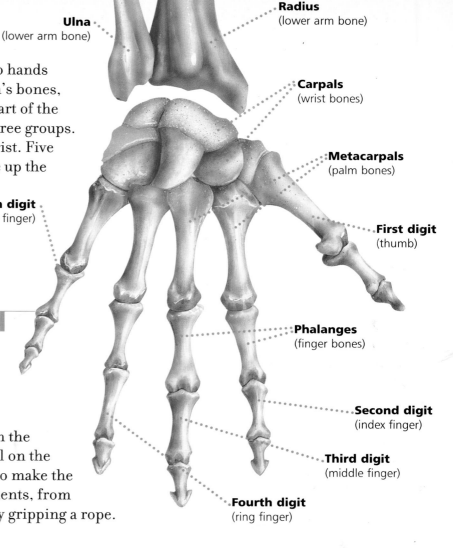

Hand bones

With 54 bones between them, the two hands contain over a quarter of the skeleton's bones, which make them the most flexible part of the body. Hand bones are divided into three groups. Two rows of eight carpals form the wrist. Five long bones, called metacarpals, make up the palm. Fourteen phalanges (three in each finger and two in the thumb) form the highly bendy and movable digits – the fingers and thumbs.

Ulna
(lower arm bone)

Radius
(lower arm bone)

Carpals
(wrist bones)

Metacarpals
(palm bones)

First digit
(thumb)

Fifth digit
(little finger)

Phalanges
(finger bones)

Second digit
(index finger)

Third digit
(middle finger)

Fourth digit
(ring finger)

Hand bones

A total of 27 bones fit together to make each hand. Some of the carpals (wrist bones) form the wrist joint with the radius and ulna.

Versatile hands

The brain controls over 30 muscles in the lower arm and in the hand. These pull on the bones of the wrist, palm and fingers to make the hand perform a wide range of movements, from delicately threading a needle to firmly gripping a rope.

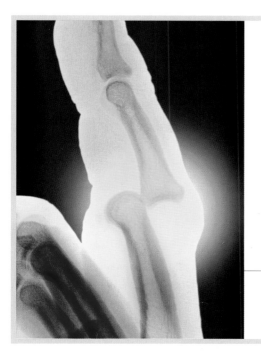

DISLOCATED BONES

In your skeleton, the bones are held firmly together by tough 'straps' called ligaments (see page 21), and by muscles. But a sudden wrench or sharp blow – perhaps caused by a fall – can force bones apart, sometimes damaging a muscle's ligaments in the process. This action is called dislocation. It happens most commonly to finger and thumb bones, and to the top of the humerus in the shoulder. Doctors can put the bones back into their correct position to ensure that no further damage occurs.

Out of place

This coloured X-ray shows clearly how two finger bones have been dislocated by being forced out of line.

The hips link the legs to
the rest of the skeleton

The hips, or pelvis, are formed by a bowl-shaped ring of bones that connects the legs to the backbone, supports and protects organs in the abdomen, and allows us to stand and move on two legs. The shape of the pelvis in adult males and females is different.

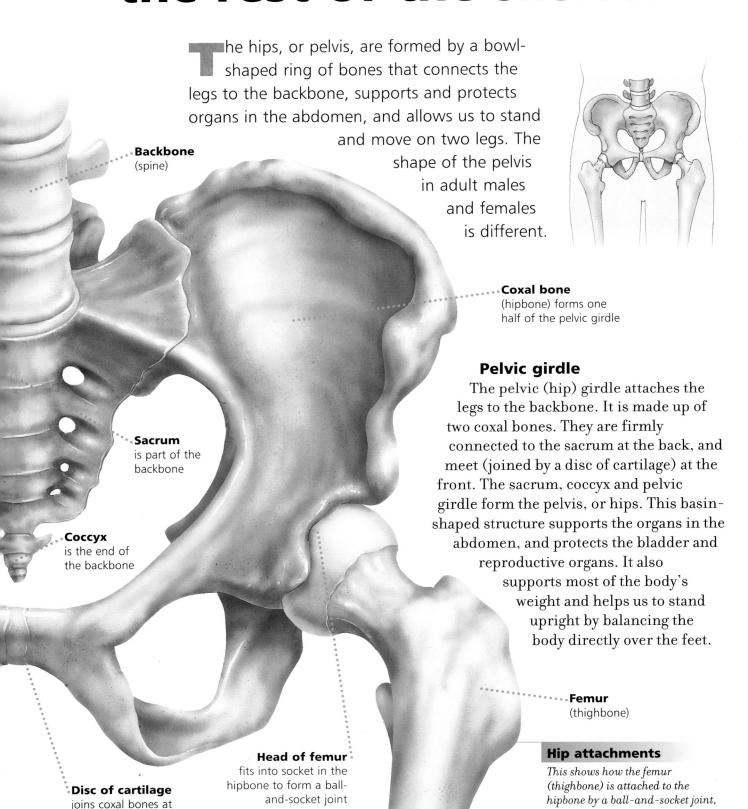

Backbone
(spine)

Coxal bone
(hipbone) forms one half of the pelvic girdle

Pelvic girdle

The pelvic (hip) girdle attaches the legs to the backbone. It is made up of two coxal bones. They are firmly connected to the sacrum at the back, and meet (joined by a disc of cartilage) at the front. The sacrum, coccyx and pelvic girdle form the pelvis, or hips. This basin-shaped structure supports the organs in the abdomen, and protects the bladder and reproductive organs. It also supports most of the body's weight and helps us to stand upright by balancing the body directly over the feet.

Sacrum
is part of the backbone

Coccyx
is the end of the backbone

Femur
(thighbone)

Head of femur
fits into socket in the hipbone to form a ball-and-socket joint

Disc of cartilage
joins coxal bones at the front

Hip attachments

This shows how the femur (thighbone) is attached to the hipbone by a ball-and-socket joint, and how the pelvic girdle is anchored to the sacrum by the coxal bones.

Hipbones

Each of the two coxal bones that make up the pelvic girdle is actually made up of three bones called the ilium, ischium and pubis. In young children these bones are separate, but in adults they are fused together. When we put our hands on our hips they rest on top of the broad ilium. The rear of the hipbone is formed by the ischium, while the front is formed by the pubis. Where the three bones meet they form the socket into which the head of the femur fits.

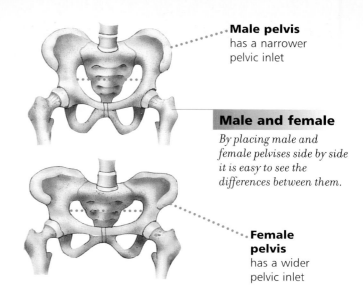

Male pelvis
has a narrower
pelvic inlet

Male and female
By placing male and female pelvises side by side it is easy to see the differences between them.

Female pelvis
has a wider
pelvic inlet

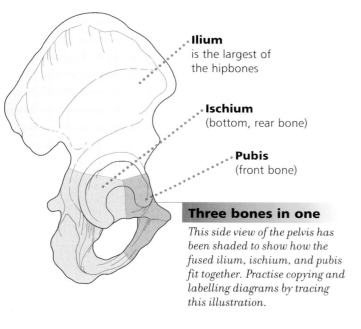

Ilium
is the largest of
the hipbones

Ischium
(bottom, rear bone)

Pubis
(front bone)

Three bones in one
This side view of the pelvis has been shaded to show how the fused ilium, ischium, and pubis fit together. Practise copying and labelling diagrams by tracing this illustration.

Pelvic differences

To the untrained eye, one skeleton looks much like another regardless of whether it once belonged to a male or female. But an expert will be able immediately to tell the sex of a skeleton by looking at its pelvis. A woman's pelvis is shallower and broader than a man's and has a wider central opening, or pelvic inlet. A woman's pelvis needs to be wider and roomier to provide enough space for a baby's head to pass through as it is being born.

HIP REPLACEMENT

Joints between bones can be damaged by disease, such as arthritis, and injury. In the past a person with a damaged hip joint (found between the femur and the hipbone) would have lost the ability to walk. But today, doctors carry out an operation called a hip replacement. The weakened ball-shaped head of the femur is removed and replaced by an artificial ball. The hip socket is lined with plastic to make sure the new joint moves smoothly.

Artificial joint
This X-ray shows an artificial hip joint made by replacing the top of the femur and the inside of the socket in the pelvic girdle.

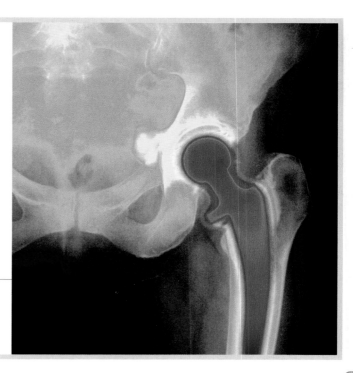

The legs and feet support and
move the body

The leg bones, which include the largest and strongest in the body, support and move the body. The feet help us to balance and stay upright, and help to push the body off the ground whenever we move.

Upper leg

Bones in the legs are arranged in a similar way to that of the arms (see pages 14–15), but they are longer, thicker and stronger, because they have to support all of the body's weight. Inside the upper leg, or thigh, is the femur (thighbone) – the biggest, strongest bone in the body. Its rounded head forms a joint with the pelvic girdle, while its lower end has a grooved surface that forms the knee joint with the tibia (shinbone).

Tibia
(shinbone)

Fibula
smaller bone of the lower leg

Talus
forms the ankle joint with the tibia and fibula

Pelvic girdle
attaches the legs to the rest of the skeleton

Femur
(thighbone)

Knee joint
between the femur and tibia

Tibia
(shinbone)

Ankle joint
between the lower leg bones and the tarsals

Strong support

The bones of the legs have to support the weight of the upper body, which is why they are so strong.

Lower leg

The tibia and fibula in the lower leg help to carry the body's weight. Together, at their lower end, the tibia and fibula form a flexible joint with the ankle bones of the foot.

Tightly linked

The bones in the foot are tightly linked by tough ligaments. They help to balance the weight of the body.

Calcaneus
(heel bone) is the largest tarsal

Tarsals
(anklebones)

Metatarsals
(sole bones)

Bone arrangement

The arrangement of bones in the feet is similar to that found in the hands. There are 26 bones in each foot (one less than in the hand) including seven tarsals, five metatarsals and 14 phalanges.

Starting blocks

Feet give us the perfect start. Muscles pull on foot and leg bones to make us walk, run and jump.

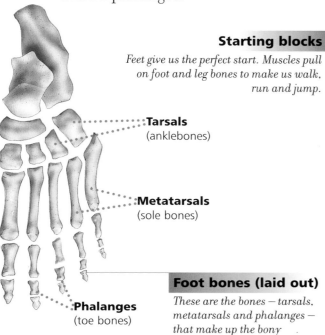

Tarsals
(anklebones)

Metatarsals
(sole bones)

Phalanges
(toe bones)

Foot bones (laid out)

These are the bones – tarsals, metatarsals and phalanges – that make up the bony framework of each foot.

Spring into action

Feet are hard workers. They have to be strong enough to carry the body's weight when we stand, walk or run and to help us balance whether we are moving or standing still on level and uneven surfaces. They work like flexible levers, bending at the ankle, and using the toes to push the body off the ground whenever we move forwards. Feet are less flexible than the hands but good at supporting, balancing and moving.

MAKING FOOTPRINTS

Next time you get out of a swimming pool look at the footprints you leave behind – they are not 'flat'. That is because only part of your foot touches the ground. The underside of each one is curved into a flexible arch. This is formed by the metatarsal bones, which are pulled upwards by ligaments and muscles. The arches act like springs, absorbing impact during walking and running, and help to spread out body weight.

Flexible arch

As this footprint shows, because of its flexible arch not all of the foot's lower surface touches the ground when we walk.

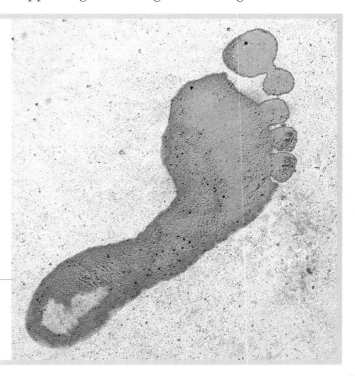

Joints give the skeleton flexibility
and allow it to move

Wherever two or more bones meet – such as in the elbow or knee – they form a joint. Without joints the skeleton would be completely stiff and unable to bend or move. Most joints, called synovial joints, move easily and freely. Others allow less movement, and a few do not move at all.

Ligament
strengthens joint

Bone

Joint capsule
holds joint together

Synovial membrane
produces synovial fluid

Synovial fluid
lubricates joints

Cartilage
covers end of bone

Inside a joint

This section through the knee, a 'typical' synovial joint, shows how synovial fluid lubricates the cartilage covering the ends of bones.

Synovial joints

Most of the joints in the skeleton – such as those in the fingers, elbows, knees, shoulders and hips – are called synovial joints. The ends of the bones are covered and protected by a thin layer of hard, smooth, slippery cartilage. Holding the joint together is a strong joint capsule that is reinforced on the outside by tough ligaments (see opposite). Its inner layer, the synovial membrane, produces synovial fluid.

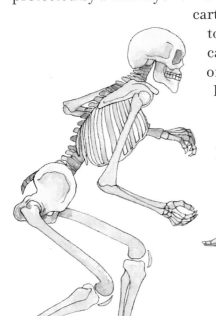

Moveable joints

Most of the body's joints move freely. This allows the skeleton – and the body – to perform an incredible range of movements.

Synovial fluid

Synovial fluid is as thick as egg white and is found in a small cavity between bone ends. It makes the cartilage even more slippery, so the bone ends slide over each other without scraping when we move.

Ligaments

Without ligaments, the body's joints would fall apart. These strong 'straps' hold neighbouring bones together so they are not pulled apart every time we move. Some ligaments hold bone together so tightly that only a small amount of movement is possible, while other ligaments are looser and allow much freer movement. Despite their great strength, ligaments sometimes tear, especially during intense exercise.

Limited movement

Some of the body's joints only allow for a little movement, or even no movement at all. The cartilage discs between vertebrae in the backbone, for example, allow limited movement, but together make the backbone very flexible (see page 12). The bones that make up the skull are locked together by immovable joints called sutures (see below and page 10).

Bendy back

A gymnast's flexible backbone enables her to perform movement such as these.

SKULL JOINTS

The bones that make up the skull join together like pieces of a jigsaw puzzle. Take two pieces of jigsaw and fit them together on a flat surface. Hold each piece with one hand and try to move the pieces against each other. There is very little movement, if any, because the curved edges of the jigsaw pieces fit together tightly. This is exactly what happens in the skull where sutures hold bones together very tightly.

Locked together

These jigsaw pieces demonstrate how skull bones lock tightly together.

Different types of joint produce
different movements

There are several different types of free-moving, or synovial, joints in the body. Each type is capable of producing a different form of movement. Together, these joints allow humans to carry out a wide range of movements.

Types of synovial joints

There are six types of synovial joints: ball-and-socket, hinge, pivot, gliding, condyloid and saddle. The movement each one produces depends on the shapes of the bone ends in the joint, and the way those ends fit together.

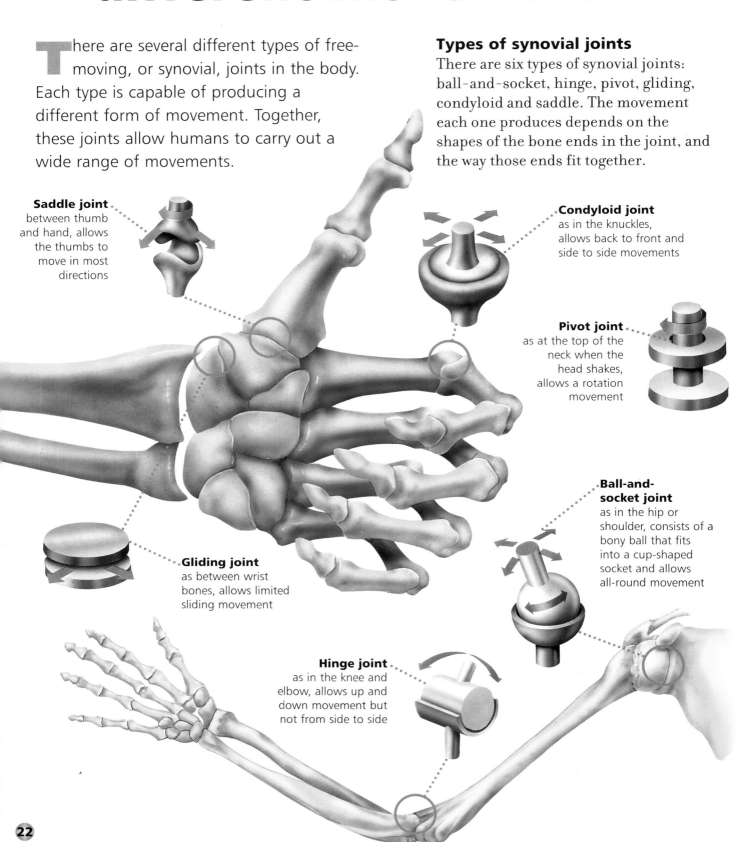

Saddle joint
between thumb and hand, allows the thumbs to move in most directions

Condyloid joint
as in the knuckles, allows back to front and side to side movements

Pivot joint
as at the top of the neck when the head shakes, allows a rotation movement

Gliding joint
as between wrist bones, allows limited sliding movement

Ball-and-socket joint
as in the hip or shoulder, consists of a bony ball that fits into a cup-shaped socket and allows all-round movement

Hinge joint
as in the knee and elbow, allows up and down movement but not from side to side

LOOKING INSIDE JOINTS

Doctors use a tube-like instrument called an endoscope to look inside the body to check that everything is working properly. A special type of endoscope, called an arthroscope, is used to look inside joints to find out if anything is wrong with them. The knee joint, for example, may have a torn ligament or bits of broken off cartilage that cause pain and stiffness. The doctor inserts the arthroscope tube through a very small cut made in the skin over the knee.

Inside view

This view inside the knee joint was taken using an arthroscope.

Body movements

Together, the different types of joint, the bones and the muscles that pull them allow the body to perform a range of movements. These are given special names by doctors and physiotherapists. Flexing, or bending, a joint brings bones closer together, while extending straightens it, moving bones further apart. Adduction moves a body part, such as an arm, away from the body (out to the side), while abduction brings it back. Depression moves a body part, such as the jaw, downwards, while elevation pulls it up.

On the move

To pull her through the water, this swimmer extends (straightens) her arms before pulling them back (by flexion and adduction).

Bones grow through infancy
to adolescence

Before we are born, our skeleton is built of flexible cartilage, the same material that supports the nose and ears. As we grow before and after birth, the cartilage is gradually replaced by much harder bone.

1. Ossification gives each cartilage 'bone' a shaft, and either a hollow centre or one filled with spongy bone.

Original cartilage 'bone'

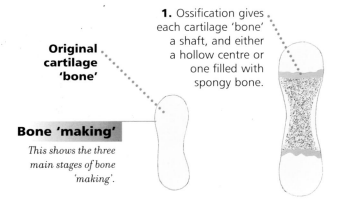

Bone 'making'
This shows the three main stages of bone 'making'.

2. After birth, the cartilage ends are gradually replaced by bone, but a band of cartilage remains to allow bones to grow longer.

3. In later childhood nearly all the cartilage has been replaced.

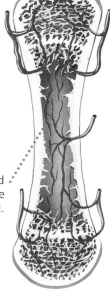

Making bones
At the beginning of development inside the uterus, we have a skeleton made of cartilage. As this cartilage skeleton enlarges, cells called osteoblasts ('bone builders') appear in the middle part of each cartilage 'bone' and produce bone in the same shape as the cartilage template. This process is called ossification ('bone-making').

From baby to adult
The X-rays below of the hands of a one-year-old, three-year-old, and 13-year-old child, and a 20-year-old adult, show how bones develop as we get older. In the youngest children (left) there are spaces between the bones, and between the middle and ends of bones, showing areas filled by cartilage. These are gradually replaced by bone as we get older (right).

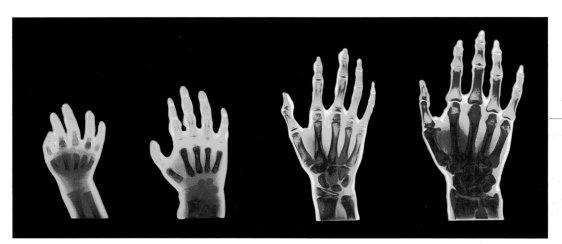

Bone growth
This sequence of coloured X-rays shows how bone replaces the cartilage 'bones'.

Growing skull

When a baby is born, his or her skull bones are linked by softer membranes called fontanelles. Fontanelles allow the skull to be squeezed without damage as a baby is born. They also allow the skull to expand to make room inside for the growing brain. By the time the child is 18 months old, the fontanelles have been replaced by bone.

Fontanelles

This X-ray of a baby's head shows the fontanelles between the skull bones.

Face formation

In infancy, the cranium, which surrounds the brain, is large in proportion to the rest of the body. This is because the brain inside is also very large. However, a child's facial bones, which form the face, are much smaller. In late childhood and early adolescence the facial bones grow larger, causing the change from the face of a child to one of an adult.

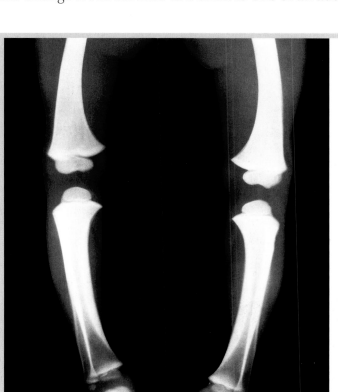

CURVED BONES

To develop properly, a child's bones need the right amount of calcium. If bones do not get enough calcium they become softer than normal, and the leg bones start to bend outwards under the body's weight (shown left). This is what happens as a result of a disease called rickets. It is caused when a child's diet lacks vitamin D, which is found in fish oils, egg yolk, butter, milk and liver – and is produced in the skin by sunlight. Vitamin D enables the body to take in calcium from food. Today, rickets is rare in Western countries, but it still occurs in countries where poverty is widespread.

Bones repair themselves naturally after **they are broken**

Bones may be hard, strong, and able to withstand great stresses, but sometimes a fall or other accident puts so much force on a bone that it breaks, or fractures. However, as living organs, bones are able to repair themselves, although they may benefit from medical help to ensure that they are set straight.

Broken bones

There are two main types of fracture. In an open or compound fracture, one or more broken bone ends stick out through the skin. In a closed or simple fracture they do not. In a bad break, especially a compound fracture, the broken bone ends need to be realigned (lined up as they would normally be) by a doctor so that they heal properly.

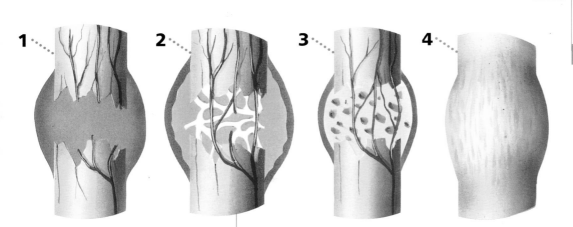

Compound fracture

This coloured X-ray shows a compound fracture of both lower arm bones, with the radius (upper bone) sticking through the skin.

Stages of healing

Bones repair themselves in a slow process – shown here are four stages.

Repair process

The picture sequence above shows how broken bones repair themselves. Soon after a fracture has happened, blood clots around the break (1) to seal off damaged blood vessels. Then (2) the periosteum (the membrane that covers bones) is replaced, and cartilage is produced to hold the broken ends together. Over the next few weeks, (3) bone replaces the cartilage. Finally, (4) the bone is repaired, leaving only a small bulge marking the original fracture.

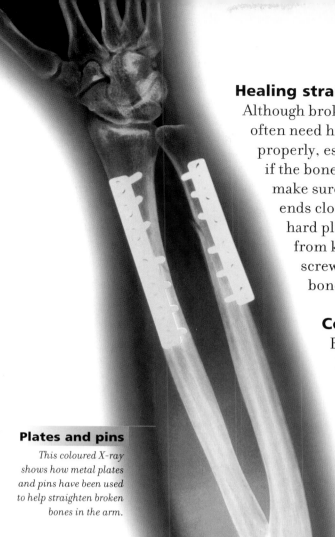

Healing straight

Although broken bones mend themselves naturally, they often need help from doctors to make sure they heal properly, especially arm and leg bones. Recovery is helped if the bones are kept still and in the correct position (to make sure repairs are not crooked) and with broken ends close to each other. This can be achieved using a hard plaster cast, which also protects the fracture from knocks. In more severe cases, metal pins or screws may be used to hold fractured arm or leg bones in place.

Constant reshaping

Bones may appear to be solid and unchanging, but they actually change shape constantly. Cells called osteoclasts ('bone breakers') break down bone, and osteoblasts ('bone builders') build it up. Bones 'reshape' according to stresses and strains put on them by our body weight as we move, so that they continue to support our body in the best way. This is why regular exercise helps to keep our bones healthy.

Plates and pins

This coloured X-ray shows how metal plates and pins have been used to help straighten broken bones in the arm.

OSTEOPOROSIS

As you get older your bones naturally lose some calcium and collagen, and become lighter and weaker. But in some people, mainly those who are elderly, the bones become very weak and can break easily. This condition is called osteoporosis ('holey bones'). People with osteoporosis can easily break their femur or wrist in falls. In some cases, vertebrae in a person's backbone crumble and collapse, so they slowly become shorter.

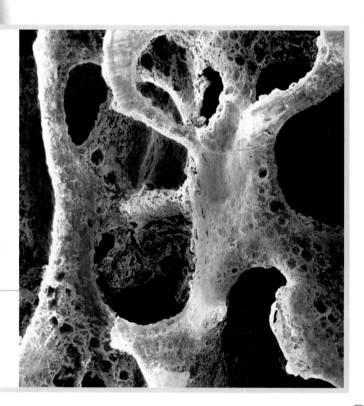

Brittle bones

This micrograph of spongy bone taken from someone with osteoporosis shows clearly how weak and brittle the structure is compared to normal spongy bone (see pages 8–9).

Old bones can help us
understand the past

The hard parts of bones, along with the teeth, can remain for thousands of years after death. These bony remains help us to understand how our ancient relatives lived, and also how we are descended from ape-like ancestors that lived millions of years ago. They also provide evidence that can help to solve recent and ancient mysteries.

Uncovering the past

After death it is the hard mineral part of bone that remains. Over hundreds of thousands of years this is replaced (in buried bones) by rock minerals to form a fossil.

Ancient bones can provide many clues to both archaeologists and scientists about how ancient people lived, what they ate, what injuries they may have sustained and if they suffered from any diseases.

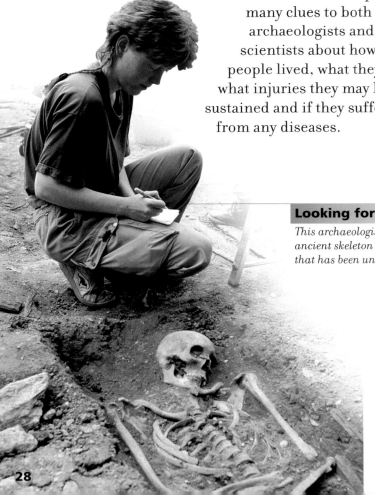

Looking for clues

This archaeologist is examining an ancient skeleton buried in a grave that has been uncovered.

Ancient bones

These fossilised bones belong to 'Lucy' a specimen of Australopithecus afarensis, an ancient African human relative that could walk on two legs.

Early humans

The earliest ape-like humans — our distant ancestors — appeared in Africa about 6 million years ago and had the ability to walk on two legs. Since then, a number of human species, such as fire-making *Homo erectus*, have appeared and died out. In the long process of human evolution (development) only one species remains in existence today — us (*Homo sapiens*).

Bigger brains

Walking on two legs rather than four meant that ancient human relatives could use their hands to pick up and use objects. It also enabled them to survey their surroundings and detect possible prey and approaching danger. To use these new abilities, humans developed bigger brains and became more intelligent. By looking at a series of skulls from about 3 million years ago to the present day we can see that the cranium has become larger as the brain has enlarged.

Dating bones

Where skeletons are hundreds of years old, scientists and archaeologists use clues, such as buried personal items, to work out the date of bones. But where human bones, or ancient human relatives, are thousands of years old, scientists use different methods, such as radioisotope dating. Radioisotopes are substances in bones that gradually break down over a set period of time.

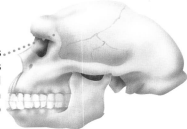

Australopithecus afarensis
lived around 3 million years ago

Homo erectus
lived around 1.8 million years ago

Homo sapiens
modern humans

Changing skulls

These skulls of Australopithecus afarensis, Homo erectus and modern humans show the increase in size of the cranium and — therefore — the brain.

FORENSIC SCULPTING

Forensic sculptors are artists who also have a detailed understanding of anatomy, the structure of the body. They use their skills to recreate the head and face of an unidentified dead person using the bones of the skull as a starting point. This technique helps archaeologists understand what ancient faces looked like, and can help the police identify people who have died more recently.

Rebuilding a face

The forensic sculptor uses modelling clay to rebuild the muscles of the head and face. Then a thin layer of clay is applied on top of the 'muscles' to form the 'skin', so recreating the face that the person once had.

Glossary

Abdomen A part of the body between the chest and the hips.

Arthritis The name for a group of diseases that cause stiffness and pain in joints.

Australopithecus afarensis An ancient ape-like human relative that lived in Africa 5 – 2 million years ago.

Blood clot The solidifying of blood that occurs at a wound to prevent blood loss.

Blood vessel A tube, such as an artery, vein, or capillary, that carries blood through the body.

Calcium phosphate The substance found in bone, which gives bone its hardness.

Cell One of trillions of tiny living units that make up the human body.

Collagen Tough protein fibres that give bone, and other tissues such as cartilage, great strength and flexibility.

Cranium The domed part of the skull that protects the brain.

Endoscope A flexible viewing instrument used by doctors to look inside the body.

Evolution The gradual change in living things over many generations which gives rise to new species (types).

Exoskeleton The harder outer covering, or skeleton, found in many animals including insects, such as beetles, and crustaceans, such as crabs.

Fossil The ancient remains of a living thing, such as a bone, found preserved as rock.

Girdle A ring of bones that attaches either the arms or legs to the rest of the skeleton.

Homo erectus The ancient human relative that lived in Africa, Europe and Asia 1.7 million to 250,000 years ago.

Joint The part of the skeleton where two or more bones meet.

Kidney One of a pair of organs that removes wastes from the blood in the form of urine.

Ligament Tough strap that holds bones together in a joint.

Lung One of a pair of organs in the chest that take oxygen into the body.

Mammals A group of animals, including humans, monkeys, bats and rabbits, that have fur, are warm-blooded and feed their young with milk.

Micrograph An image taken using a high-powered microscope.

Muscle The body tissue that contracts to pull bones and move the body.

Organ A body part, such as a bone, that is made up of two or more types of tissues and which has a specific job to do.

Osteoblast A cell that builds up bone tissue.

Osteoclast A cell that breaks down bone tissue.

Osteocyte A bone cell that maintains bone tissue.

Oxygen The gas found in the air that is needed by cells to release from food the energy that is necessary for life.

Periosteum The membrane that covers the outside of bones and contains blood vessels.

Radioactive Substances that break down naturally and give off tiny particles in the form of radiation.

Red blood cells Disc-shaped cells, made by red bone marrow and found in the blood, that carry oxygen to all body cells.

Spinal cord A column of nervous tissue that runs down the back, through the backbone, and carries nerve messages between brain and body.

Suture A joint found between skull bones that does not allow any movement.

Tendon A cord or sheet of tough tissue that connects muscles to the bones that they move.

Tissue A collection of the same, or similar, cells that work together to perform a specific task.

Vitamin One of a group of over 13 substances, including vitamin D, needed in small amounts in a person's diet to make the body work normally.

White blood cells Cells produced by red bone marrow that are carried by the blood and help defend the body against germs.

Find out more

These are just some of the websites where you can find out more information about the human skeleton. Many of the websites also provide information and illustrations about other systems and processes of the human body.

Note to parents and teachers
Every effort has been made by the Publishers to ensure that these websites are suitable for children; that they are of the highest educational value, and that they contain no inappropriate or offensive material. However, because of the nature of the Internet, it is impossible to guarantee that the contents of these sites will not be altered. We strongly advise that Internet access is supervised by a responsible adult.

www.brainpop.com/heal th/skeletalsystem
Visit this website for quizzes, movies and fascinating facts about bones and the skeleton.

www.medtropolis.com/ VBody.asp
Click on 'Skeleton' on this virtual body website to get a guided tour of bones, and the chance to build your own skeleton.

http://health.howstuff works.com/x-ray.htm
Find out about Wilhelm Roentgen, his discovery of X-rays and how X-rays work.

www.gwc.maricopa.edu/ class/bio201/skull/skull tt.htm
Have fun with the skull and identify its bones at the same time.

www.pbs.org/wgbh/evol ution/humans/riddle/
Check out the 'Riddle of the Bones' on this website to discover more about our earliest human relatives.

http://yucky.kids.discov ery.com/flash/body/pg0 00124.html
Find out lots of interesting facts about bones from the yuckiest site on the Internet.

www.bbc.co.uk/science/ humanbody/body/index. shtml
For lots of information about the skeleton, joints and bone growth.

www.kidshealth.org/kid /body
Click on bones to read 'The Big Story of Bones' and discover more about your skeleton.

Index